social studies in the open classroom: a practical guide

social studies

in the open classroom:

a practical guide

EVELYN BERGER AND BONNIE A. WINTERS

TEACHERS COLLEGE PRESS
Teachers College, Columbia University
New York and London

Photographs courtesy of
Office of Public Information
Teachers College, Columbia University

Cover design by **dorothy.**

Manufactured in the United States of America

contents

social studies in the open classroom: a practical guide

social studies—
a key factor in the open classroom

The proverb attributed to the Chinese and quoted in the Carnegie report is a succinct statement of the philosophy of the open classroom. "I listen and I forget; I see and I remember; I do and I understand." This suggestion of action and involvement, exemplifying the concept of education as a social experience, as "living," is the core of the open classroom. In the enriched and carefully planned environment of an open classroom, children can learn by themselves or from each other in a variety of real-life situations.

Is it not an obvious extension of this idea to suggest that social studies is in fact an experience in living? Social studies is by definition social education—a series of social experiences whose goal is understanding our own lives and the lives of other people. Social studies is *people*, and in the open classroom each child is a unique person, endowed with the ability to think and act both as an individual and as a group member. *People*—their individual rights and privileges, their adjustment to each other and to their world, and their working out of mutual problems—are the shared goals of a good social studies program and a successful open classroom. What better way, then, to initiate or expand your open classroom than through social studies?

Some open classrooms neglect social studies, possibly because of the feeling that the social situation existing in the classroom provides adequate "social" studies. Much emphasis has been given to math, science, and language disciplines; art, music, and physical education have found their place in the open classroom because they seem to lend themselves to the program by virtue of their use of manipulative devices and readily available materials and equipment. However, in terms of achievable goals, no other aspect of an elementary school curriculum is as closely tied to the open classroom concept as is social studies.

On the following page, for purposes of comparison, are some suggested goals for (1) any open classroom, and (2) any social studies program. As you read and interpret them, it will become increasingly clear that social studies is indeed an ideal vehicle for the development of an open classroom.

Dr. Leonard Kenworthy, in *Social Studies for the Seventies*, describes the task of a social studies teacher as the discovery and development of every child's abilities so that he or she may comprehend himself or herself and other human beings, cope with life more effectively, contribute to society in his or her own way, help to change society, enjoy it, and share in its benefits. Dr. Kenworthy could as well have been setting down the goals of a teacher in the microcosm of life that is an open classroom.

Whatever your current interest in the open classroom may be, we will try to meet your needs in this book. You may now be planning to launch an open classroom for the first time; perhaps you would like to enrich the social studies program in your present open classroom; or you may just be hoping for an opportunity to implement the ideas you can gather about open classrooms.

In any case, there are a few cautions to keep in mind as we

GOALS OF AN OPEN CLASSROOM

GOALS OF A SOCIAL STUDIES PROGRAM

- To recognize each child as a unique individual, with the ability to think and act in his own way.

- To recognize the dignity and worth of each individual.

- To encourage each child to learn about the world around him.

- To understand our environment and people's dependence on each other.

- To use a variety of materials so that children can discover that there are often many ways of doing the same thing.

- To develop the ability to make choices, based on experience, comparisons, and the exercise of judgment.

- To encourage children to try, to discover, to experiment, even to make mistakes without anxiety or apprehension.

- To develop the skills that encourage active, productive social behavior.

- To develop a respect and understanding of other people's needs and desires.

- To acquire knowledge that is pertinent and applicable to life situations.

- To develop concern and responsibility for the group.

- To accept responsibility for oneself and one's group.

---

proceed to the specifics of a social studies program in an open classroom.

Consider carefully the social studies program in your school. Most school systems have established specific social studies programs for each grade level. In establishing an open classroom, certain concessions need to be made by supervisors and principals in terms of relaxing the rigidity of program requirements. Try not to be tied to a preestablished sequence in your program. The "teachable moment," a situation in which a child or group of children have an experience that generates an interest in learning about a specific area, is an integral part of an open classroom and cannot be compromised; it is at such moments that interest and motivation are at their height. Children must be allowed freedom of choice in their efforts if their activities are to be meaningful. Your control of the situation comes from the fact that you plan and provide the "enriched environment"; you supply the materials; you collect the books, maps, and realia relating to the historical period, geographic area, or cultural activity being studied. Your control also comes from your planning of suggested tasks—ideas and activities whose implementation will initially take the children into fields that may be a required part of your program. You should make it clear that if a child develops a particular interest as a result of some investigation, he will be allowed free rein in further exploration of that interest even if it exceeds the original limits of your program. For instance, in a study of Tanzania, a student may become interested in the Leakey discoveries and want to investigate other archaeological discoveries. Certainly he should be encouraged and assisted in this effort, though it may not fulfill specific program requirements. How many budding anthropologists or architects or clothes designers have been lost to the world because the development of their interests or talents did not fit into a required school program?

Although whole-class activities are rare in an open classroom, they should certainly not be completely eliminated. These large-group situations can meet certain needs and many important skills can be learned from them: audience conduct, as well as many speaking and listening skills, are most appropriately presented in this kind of setting. The difference between a traditional and an open class is in the move away from the authoritarian teacher-figure to a large-group situation in which children themselves hold the position of teacher or speaker. If the group wants to meet together, and members of the group have information or questions to share, then a whole-class meeting serves to reinforce the goal of developing group responsibility. Particularly at the start of the school year, when your open classroom is just being launched, it may be useful to hold short whole-class meetings at the beginning of each day. At this time, new suggested tasks can be introduced, questions can be answered, and individual and group plans for the day can be made. Some teachers may want to use schedule sheets, marked off in half-hour periods, so that each child can plan a tentative schedule for his own day. If you decide to use schedules, be sure that the children realize they are not irrevocably tied to any schedule, even one they plan themselves. And any planned activity that proves especially interesting can certainly be continued beyond its scheduled time.

Although mobility, communication, and interpersonal relationships are essential parts of a social studies program in an open classroom, the "social" aspect must not collapse into chaos. An open classroom is not chaotic, disruptive, or purposeless. It is "organized freedom": freedom with responsibility—responsibility for one's own actions and for the needs and desires of the group. If your classroom is functioning within the established goals, there will be a format—a structure, if you will—that meets these goals. And if the goals and the structure are mutually acceptable to the children and to you, as guide and leader, then there will be "organized freedom."

Because the open classroom utilizes all teachable moments, you must be prepared to be a jack-of-all-trades in the social studies. The situation may require you to be an anthropologist one day, a sociologist the next. And in future unpredictable situations, you may well be asked to become an instant expert in history, economics, political science, or geography. But like the proverbial jack-of-all-trades, you may very likely also be master of none. Consequently, your social studies program each day will probably incorporate your activity as a *learner,* and put you into a situation that requires you to accept the fact that you have only limited knowledge of many areas. Many times in an open classroom you may find yourself saying, "Why don't *we* investigate . . . ?" You and the children are co-learners, co-investigators, co-workers in almost every aspect of your program.

Another point to consider is the fact that the fun and apparent relaxation of an open classroom result from careful planning on your part. Teaching in an open classroom is not an easy job. Gratifying and rewarding, yes; easy, definitely not. Collecting materials and planning suggested tasks for individuals and for groups is a complex job. Many of your own experiences and life situations can become useful parts of your classroom. Trips and cultural activities, magazine and newspaper articles, radio and television programs, and interesting people you may meet can be shared, investigated, observed, listened to, read about, and discussed with your students. Anything that is a part of living can be integrated into an open classroom. And a social studies program in your open classroom makes you a recycler of all kinds of things that now become a useful part of your class activity. There will no longer be any need to say, "Wait until December when we study about_____and then we'll answer your question."

With these cautions in mind, we now consider the planning and implementation of a social studies program in your open classroom. Although there are many possible suggestions, your choice among them depends upon the specific goals that you set for your program; the age and abilities of your students; their interests and desires from day to day; the availability of specific materials; and the degree of flexibility in your prescribed social studies program.

The functioning of any aspect of your open classroom, including your social studies program, is markedly improved if your particular school situation provides for the use of aides (volunteer or paid) from the community, and student teachers from nearby colleges. Final responsibility for all programs belongs to the classroom teacher. The addition of other adults to your classroom will free you for more individual and small-group learning experiences with the children. Aides and students can work with you in planning activities, and can supplement your skills with their own specialities and interests. High school students who plan to attend a teacher training college can be useful helpers in your class. Some high schools have senior-year work experience programs that could supply your class with willing workers. Even upper-grade students in your own school can be asked to share experiences or interests with groups of children from your class. One goal of a social studies program in an open classroom is to be an experience in living; contacts with many people, under your guidance and direction, add depth and breadth to your program.

Our next section, How to Begin, discusses the physical arrangement of your room. In later chapters, we explain techniques that you can use in developing your program. Many of these can be adapted to suit the needs of any group, or they may just give you some clues to help you develop your own ideas. Your enthusiasm, skill, and ingenuity are the most important ingredients for a successful social studies program in an open classroom. As always, you, as the teacher, hold the key to the ultimate success of any program in your classroom.

how to begin

Having accepted the pedagogical value of a social studies program in an open classroom, your next question will be the obvious "How shall I begin?" As with all meaningful classroom innovations, implementation of a social studies program depends largely upon the needs of your group. But there are some general guidelines that may be useful to you; they can be adapted to your particular situation. Both of the writers have conducted open classrooms, but in very different situations, each with very different needs. Just as each child is unique, so particular groups of children and particular school situations are unique.

There are a great many possibilities for the physical arrangement of your open classroom for social studies. Decisions about the room arrangements will depend upon a variety of factors.

- The size of the room.
- The number of children in the group.
- The availability of furnishings such as dividers, carrels (en-

closed study cubicles), tables, chairs, cushions, and rugs. These can be highly sophisticated or improvised. The success of your program does not depend upon the cost of these materials, although items made commercially for a specific purpose do tend to be more substantial and more convenient. Carrels can be made of cardboard cartons; movable, free-standing bookcases, clothing lockers, file cabinets, or pegboards on legs make good dividers; tables can be improvised by pushing desks together. Comfortable chairs, cushions, and rug pieces can often be obtained from parents or from interested local merchants.

• The structure of the social studies program. This may mean: (a) having one interest center in your room devoted to all the social studies material and tasks; these materials and tasks can be changed and added to as your program emphasis changes; or (b) having several interest centers to encourage the children to work on as many ramifications of social studies as possible. For example, you might have several centers, each with materials and tasks about a specific family, community, or country. Or you might have centers, each with materials and tasks involving a particular cultural aspect or way of life—food, clothing, government, housing, education, recreation. In this type of structure, the children can more easily concentrate on a particular field of interest. However, if you are in a self-contained classroom, you will certainly be crowded, unless you decide, after discussion with the class, to use the entire room for social studies for limited periods of time. These decisions should always be made with the children. They should be aware of physical limitations of the room, and should consider these limitations in relation to whatever they might like to do. In this situation, the keynote, as always, should be freedom with the responsibility to decide what is best for the whole group. You can use this kind of opportunity to discuss with the children why certain activities must be curtailed or postponed because of physical limitations in the classroom. This kind of deliberation can help develop the ability to make decisions and necessary compromises in real-life situations.

If you are in a school with an open program involving several classes, you may be fortunate enough to have individual rooms equipped for each subject area (e.g. social studies, art, reading). In this case, interest centers should be set up after discussion among all the teachers involved, and be based upon the abilities and interests of the children in all the classes. Your school's prescribed social studies program determines the various possibilities for interest centers in a social studies room. You and the other teachers have to make decisions about books, other materials, and suggested tasks, based upon the answers to many questions, for example: What kind of materials are available? Does the program at your level have family, community, or national orientation? What kinds of people does it concentrate on? Do you emphasize specific periods of American history with their many ramifications? Obviously, a room or rooms especially designated for social studies can provide many opportunities for exploration not available in a self-contained classroom. But don't postpone or cancel your plans because of what seems to be a space problem. Enthusiasm and ingenuity can more than compensate for space limitations.

Having determined the most convenient physical arrangement for your room or rooms, you might draw a simple sketch, scaled to the available space. In this way, you can more readily make decisions about the items you will have room for: for example, the number and size of tables and chairs; the best location for study carrels; the best location for audiovisual equipment in relation to electric outlets. When you and your school principal have decided upon the most expedient method of meeting these needs, you can then proceed to the business of accumulating the materials to use in developing your program—the "stuff" of which your program is made.

Since social studies, especially in an open classroom, is an experience in living, it is virtually impossible to make an all-inclusive list of suggested materials. We merely suggest categories that may prove useful. With the help of your librarian or media specialist, you and the children can supplement these suggestions. Within each category, the things you select for use will depend upon your specific program, the age, ability, and interests of your class, and the availability of various items. Here, then, are some things to start collecting.

- A few copies of each of several selected social studies texts, appropriate to your grade and program. These can be used for reference.
- Any available trade books, including cookbooks, pertinent to your program; fiction related to cultures and historical periods to be studied; international songbooks and books with songs from various historical periods.
- One or more globes with current boundaries and names; atlases and maps of all kinds—political, physical, and relief maps, population distribution maps, road maps.
- Daily and Sunday newspapers; newspapers from other communities—foreign and United States; weekly newsmagazines and back and current copies of illustrated periodicals.
- Vertical files for newspaper and magazine clippings, pamphlets, brochures, free material, mounted and unmounted pictures, etc. Metal files are great and permanent; transfer files of heavy cardboard are also useful, especially those that have metal edges to make them last longer.
- Audiovisual "software"—records, filmstrips, transparencies, film loops, cassette and regular tapes—that can supplement your program. The "hardware," or machines—film and filmstrip projectors, record players, opaque and overhead projectors, radio and television sets, loop projectors, tape recorders—are most frequently used on a shared basis among many classes, although you may be one of the fortunate few whose individual rooms are equipped with some of these machines.

• Realia—handicrafts, flags, traditional clothing, stamps, coins, and currency—from areas of the world that will be investigated during the year.

• Plants and animals from other geographic areas; this may present some difficulties, but plants such as cactus and rain forest plants, and small desert animals such as gerbils and snakes, as well as tropical fish, can provide an experience related to the flora and fauna of the areas to be explored.

• Study prints, travel posters, other pictures.

• Graphs and charts of information pertinent to your program.

• A "treasure chest" of materials for improvising costumes from areas to be investigated—old sheets, large and small pieces of assorted fabrics, ribbons, lace, jewelry, wigs, feathers. Parents, friends, or local merchants may add to your collection.

• Cushions and carpet pieces for "sit-upons." Parents and interested local merchants may help to supply these.

• Large appliance cartons for making stores, puppet stages, etc.

• Mobile carts, tables, or bookshelves so that supplies of all kinds can be portable.

There are several sources of names and addresses of companies that distribute useful free materials. A few suggestions:

Educators Guide to Free Curriculum Materials in Social Studies, published annually by Educators Progress Service, Randolph, Wisc. 53956

Salisbury, Gordon. Catalog of Free Teaching Materials. P.O. Box 1075, Ventura, Calif. 93002

Wagner and Christophel. Free Learning Materials for Classroom Use. State College Extension Service, Cedar Falls, Iowa.

Embassies and information offices of most foreign countries send information about their countries on request. This material is usually useful, but some of it is promotional propaganda, and must be used with discretion.

TASK CARDS

Now we begin to make particular suggestions about how to stimulate the children and to meet your specific goals. An important technique in the implementation of many of these suggestions is the use of task cards. Before we discuss the suggestions, a general explanation of task cards might be useful to you.

Most teachers will find it convenient to write out questions or explanations of suggested activities for the children on some kind of index card. The size—and colors, if possible—of these task cards should vary, depending upon the extent of the explanation: 3 x 5 cards are useful for simple questions; 4 x 6 or 5 x 8 cards can be used when more detailed information is necessary. In any case, if you type the cards, use double or triple spacing to make them easier to read, and also to leave space for additions or corrections. If the children need some experience in reading cursive writing, use a felt-tip pen and write clearly. For children who have only beginning reading skills, some of the directions can be done with pictures or drawings. Questions and directions should be clear and specific, so that children can use the task cards without significant adult assistance. Be sure that the children understand the goal of each task and what their final product should be.

The method of storing these task cards depends upon the needs of your class and the containers that are available. A variety of baskets, boxes, and buckets provide color and interest. Choosing a task on a card from "the red bucket" or "the square bucket" or "the striped box" can add a little appeal to the work. Task cards can be used for an endless variety of ideas. All kinds of research possibilities can be suggested on task cards; riddles, questions, and puzzles can be introduced; role-playing ideas can be recommended; all sorts of problem-solving situations can be explained; art ideas can be presented. Anything that you or the children see as an interesting activity can find its way onto a task card. To help the children become oriented to the use of the task cards, it is a good idea to sort them out in some way before using them. In your social studies

interest center, for example, you might have a basket of research suggestions, a box of art ideas, and a bucket of problem-solving activities. The plan for sorting the task cards should be simple and easily understood by the children.

It is most important to change and add to the task cards continually. In social studies, of course, many changes are built into the changing emphases of your program. Some ideas can be reused by merely changing the locale. For example, research into clothing or food customs can be done for various countries; solving the problem of limited natural resources is a significant situation in many world areas; drawings of homes can be a useful and interesting activity for many historical periods and many countries. We cannot emphasize too strongly, however, the need for maintaining high interest and a sense of challenge by varying the suggestions. If the excitement of learning that is part of the open classroom is to be sustained, there must be a constant flow of ideas and materials in your classroom.

Now, to review our proposed initial steps for introducing a social studies program into your open classroom.

• Plan the physical arrangement that best meets the needs of your class and your program, keeping in mind your goals and the limitations of your school plant.

• Start to collect materials to implement your program. Be on the alert for possible sources. Since this is a program of "living," the possibilities for material are limitless.

audiovisual activities

Since much of the supplementary material available for social studies is associated with audiovisual equipment, it is important to note the importance of student involvement in all phases of these activities. Audiovisual presentations must be *their* activities, rather than demonstrations or exhibits by the teacher. Make as much audiovisual equipment as possible available to the children. At most grade levels, even the lowest, there are children who can be taught to operate some of the machines—televisions, radios, filmstrip projectors, cameras, opaque and overhead projectors, cassette recorders, record players, and other simple equipment. Often the children with sufficient manual dexterity to operate some of this equipment are those whose academic skills are less developed, and they have an opportunity to experience success in this area. Children usually respond to the responsibility of these tasks by handling the machines with great care, and often with much greater effectiveness than some teachers who are afraid of the equipment and consequently avoid using it. Some of the more complicated and delicate machines can be handled by middle- and upper-graders. In any case, the emphasis on involvement and responsibility that is so significant a goal of an open classroom should be clearly defined in activities involving audiovisual equipment.

Although almost any type of hardware can have some application to an open classroom social studies program, some kinds of audiovisual activities are more useful than others. Opaque projectors, film projectors, and other equipment that requires a darkened room limit the activities of other groups if you are confined to one room. Most sound-producing audiovisual hardware—radios, televisions, tape recorders, record players—is used most advantageously in an open classroom if a jack box, or listening station, and headphones are attached so that the entire class is not disturbed by the sound. Such a listening kit ought to be portable, perhaps placed on a rolling cart so that all parts are kept together.

The equipment available to you will also depend on the available funds. Some of the suggestions given here may be beyond your budget; there are frequently less expensive alternatives.

Previewers, for individual or small-group viewing of filmstrips, are invaluable in an open classroom. There are many types, varying widely in price. When there are more than three children in a group, it is wiser to employ a filmstrip projector and a small portable screen. A screen can be improvised by using a white sheet or piece of white butcher paper taped onto a wall.

Blank film for making **filmstrips** is available from many sources, so that children can produce their own strips, using thin felt pens or special pencils for the drawings. After the group has planned the sequence of pictures, individual children can volunteer to draw the pictures that they prefer. Before they start, draw pictures of a length of blank film on several sheets of paper, and mark off the size of the frames. (Some copying machines will make copies of a piece of actual film that you put into the machine.) The children should draft pictures on paper until they are satisfied with one, then tape the film over the finished picture and trace it. The children can write the commentary on the film itself or they can make a tape or cassette to go with it. Or they can just write out the commentary on a piece of paper and read it aloud as the strip is projected.

There are a great many good **phonograph records** of folk songs, stories, and speeches that are intended for social studies use. These can be used by individual children or small groups, and are especially good in your open classroom if you have a listening kit.

A **reel-to-reel tape recorder** or a **cassette recorder** can also be used effectively with headsets. There are many excellent commercial tapes designed to bring to life historical events, folk songs and stories, and international festivals and holidays. In addition, you may elect to make your own tapes from available social studies printed material, or from original material that you or the children have written. Children who are "turned off" to reading may listen to social studies tapes with great interest. They may even be motivated to seek out related written material to read.

Tapes and records can be used by themselves, or in conjunction with filmstrips or study prints. There are many commercial **multi-media kits** for social studies that combine cassettes or records with filmstrips or pictures. You can, of course, make your own cassettes to go with filmstrips or with pictures from magazines or newspapers.

If you have access to a **dry mount machine**, it is a good idea to mount and laminate pictures for class use. You will find that mounted pictures last much longer and are thus worth the effort. **Tapes** can be easily erased and used for new mini-lessons as you find additional pictures, and children will enjoy making their own tapes. From simple study prints to sophisticated 8-millimeter movies, children can develop numerous and varied presentations using tapes.

A small, inexpensive, easy-to-operate **camera** is a welcome addition to a class. One that also produces slides can provide many interesting activities. Children may want to cover an important event in the community, taking the camera along. Those who travel during school vacations may take along their own cameras and plan a display for the class when they return. Even children who have never ventured out of the neighborhood can produce a slide show by using a **camera copier** that makes slides from pictures drawn by the children or cut from magazines. They can also make a tape of commentary for these slides. A **Polaroid camera** is another exciting piece of classroom equipment, since children are always fascinated by taking pictures that they can look at immediately. A child who has worked on a Mexican peasant costume or an Indian sari loves to capture it on film and see instant results, and it deepens his interest and increases retention of the details involved in the activity.

If you can manage to get one, an **8-millimeter movie camera** and a **projector** can provide a good learning experience, used with or without a correlated tape. Class plays about newsworthy events or human interest stories can be captured in motion. Neighborhood ecology also makes an exciting topic for a movie with narration. You'll find most children eager to play Cecil B. DeMille.

An **overhead projector** has many uses and can be used in a lighted room with the group leader facing the group while the machine projects material on a screen or wall behind him. Since most of these projectors are operated by an on-off switch and a simple focusing device, they are easy for children to use and are excellent for many small-group activities. The conventional use of an overhead projector is with transparencies and overlays. These can be purchased commercially or made by students and teachers on individual pieces or rolls of transparent acetate or similar material. You can use felt pens or grease pencils, but be sure to check whether they are erasable or permanent. Your choice will depend upon your specific needs. Pages from books or magazines can be made into transparencies with the proper duplicating equipment, and many companies sell pictures, maps, and charts that can be used for this purpose. If you make your own transparencies, try to mount them in some kind of frame to preserve them. Certain kinds of developed x-ray films that are no longer useful as such can be washed and used for making your own transparencies. Ask your local hospital or radiologist about this possibility.

Map study can be made more interesting and meaningful with the use of transparencies and colored overlays to show growth and changes, such as America's westward expansion, or to introduce one map concept at a time. For example, an outline map of the United States might have one overlay showing the states, another showing capitals, and another showing mountains, rivers, and lakes. Many of these are available commercially; you can also purchase colored acetate sheets and make your own overlays.

There are rolls of acetate film that attach to two reels and can be rolled across the face of the overhead projector. They can be used by the children to illustrate an original story, or to draw scenes and well-known landmarks from places talked about in the social studies program. A less conventional use for the overhead projector is for shadow pictures. A child can role-play a situation, using fingers as the characters, and have the action projected on the screen. Topics for these playlets can be determined by the interests of the performers and the audience. A problem in group dynamics could be worked out through this medium. Often, children who are reluctant to express their innermost thoughts are willing to attribute these thoughts to their fingers through shadow play on an overhead projector.

An **opaque projector,** which requires a darkened room for best results, is most useful if you have an auxiliary area outside your classroom—or for occasions when the whole class uses it together. Its advantage, of course, is in projecting pictures of any opaque printed material, rather than being limited, as an overhead projector is, to transparent material. An opaque projector throws the image of whatever you place under it onto a large screen or wall. It is especially helpful for map study, for projecting pictures or printed pages from social studies-related books, and for sharing certain kinds of realia—for example, stamps, coins, and jewelry. In the past, one of its limitations was its large size, which made it cumbersome for children to handle. Now you can find portable opaque projectors that are lightweight, easy to operate, and relatively inexpensive. Some project only small items; some of them come with adapters for projecting larger items. There is even a small machine that costs less than ten dollars that can be used, for example, to project picture postcards, allowing children to share their own travel experiences. Opaque projectors of all kinds are good for projecting maps, charts, and other materials on walls or bulletin boards so that the larger projections can be traced and kept for permanent use.

The use of the **16-millimeter sound projector** and the **films** available in your school district has obvious advantages for a social studies program. Their open classroom limitations come from the need for a darkened room and some acoustical privacy. For occasions when a film has value for the whole class, or for situations where other room space is available for an interested group, this is certainly a useful medium.

A small **television set** for small-group viewing of educational network programs or worthwhile programs on commercial stations is an excellent addition to an open classroom social studies program. If your class budget will not cover this, your school may have a TV set on a mobile cart that you can borrow when you want it. After school hours there are many programs worth viewing. You might keep track of some of these on a weekly TV bulletin board. There are many possibilities, in terms of individual reports, group discussions, and other projects. The value of television for current events is obvious, both on a daily basis or to follow major news or sports events, such as an election, a space shot, or Olympic Games.

A classroom **radio** to be used with headphones is a valuable tool, especially for daily news broadcasts or special events.

An interesting piece of audiovisual hardware is a **video tape recorder,** which is rather expensive, and is more practical as a school- or system-owned item. It has the advantage of recording sight and sound simultaneously, and readying the tape for projection immediately. Video tapes can be used for recording special events or projects that will be useful for future use or to share with other classes.

One of the newer media for school use is the **film loop and projector.** The loops are short film cartridges that repeat automatically until the operator stops the process. There are many advantages to these loops, especially the silent type, in an open classroom; the sound film loops and projectors are still expensive and, naturally, add to the noise level. Children can handle this medium easily without adult help; the loops, which are almost indestructible, are most often "single concept" and can be repeated to reinforce and emphasize learnings. Loops are now available from several sources; many of them are social studies oriented, including some on human relations concepts.

One audiovisual medium that shows great promise is **microforms,** which in various ways reduce printed material to miniature size for storage. All microforms need some kind of hardware to enlarge the printed material to readable size. With the increase of available printed social studies material, microforms may well be the answer to libraries' space and storage problems. Their application to an open classroom situation is clear, since these materials are intended for individual use.

With today's great emphasis on improved technology, audiovisual hardware and software are changing constantly, and we must be alert to the new materials that will help us improve our teaching. As always, your skill and enthusiasm as the classroom teacher are the key to the success of audiovisual additions to your program.

when the children arrive

The primary emphasis of this book is on the actual implementation of your program with the children—the answer to the question, "What kinds of activities can be suggested for the children as part of a social studies program in an open classroom?" The use of the word "suggested" is deliberate, since many activities are generated by a specific interest on the part of a child or a group of children, rather than resulting directly from the teacher's instructions. The activities you suggest and the materials you provide serve as motivation and as a catalyst to encourage further involvement among your students.

The ideas we suggest here are arranged into several categories. Some are in the area of skills training: map study skills; research skills; communication and language arts skills; and arts and crafts skills. For each, we give some general thoughts and some specific ideas for implementation, incorporating suggestions to be put on

26

your task cards.* Ideas for strengthening problem-solving ability, including an explanation of role-playing and its use in an open classroom social studies program, follow the skills section. In addition, we discuss a few social studies ideas in greater detail, as examples of how to expand those aspects of your program that you consider worthy of particular emphasis on your part.

Our sorting into categories should not be interpreted in any precise fashion, since it is merely our way of applying a rather loose kind of order to a rather long list of suggestions. More important than categorizing the ideas is to use, expand, interpret, and improve them, and to develop from them your own techniques to share in turn with other teachers.

*Ideas which are ready to be presented to students with little or no adaptation appear in this type.

research skills

The teaching of research skills is, of course, basic to any school program, traditional or open class. The difficulties arise when children are sent to a library to "do a report" or "look up" something before they have any experience with basic research skills. The frustration and failure they experience can easily be avoided.

In an open classroom, where experience in research skills is provided for individuals or small groups rather than an entire class at once, a research training center is useful. The basic need is for some kind of movable furniture that can hold books and other printed material. The mobility is important; the children should be able to take the materials to the part of the room where they are needed, and move them out of the way when they are not needed. A library cart is one answer, but there are numerous possibilities for improvisation. You can put casters on one or two old classroom desks, and nail wooden strips around the edges of the desk top to keep books from falling off. Or put an orange crate on wheels.

The research training center should include a current encyclopedia set, two or three dictionaries of varied difficulty, a thesaurus (a children's one, if possible), atlases, almanacs, a collection of relevant newspaper clippings, a selection of pamphlets, free material relevant to your program, magazines, and trade and text books. With these materials, the teacher, or the school's librarian or media specialist, can provide small groups of children with research experience. It is important that these sessions be conducted in answer to the expressed need of a group of children who want to begin a research project. In the training center, they can help each other learn how to alphabetize, use an index and table of contents, scan and skim for information, take notes, and proofread. Your responsibility, in addition to acting as guide and co-learner, is to supply material for additional practice in those skills for which the children may need reinforcement.

When children have had some experience with basic research skills, they can move, individually or in small groups, to your school library or media center, or to the public library, to use additional printed material, as well as audiovisual equipment and materials. Here, the skills of locating, gathering, organizing, and evaluating information are further reinforced. For reluctant or problem readers, study prints, cassettes, or records can be used. You can mount (or dry mount, if your school has the equipment) magazine pictures, so that you have a permanent picture collection. This is especially useful for slower children doing research.

One of the simpler tasks for the reinforcement of research skills is to investigate the biographies of famous people. You can suggest several choices, and have children make their own selections, based upon their interests. For example, sports-minded youngsters might do some research about Paavo Nurmi, while those who are interested in music could investigate the life of Jean Sibelius: both would achieve significant goals in a study of Finland. Biographical material is usually readily available and is excellent for establishing such skills as determining sequence of events and selecting significant details. However, it should be kept in mind that the goal of biographical research is to determine the reasons for the importance of the individual, his special contribution to his group, and his effect there and upon people in other groups. The emphasis, in other words, should be on the uniqueness of the individual, rather than on the "where and when" facts that are too often the sole content of biographical research reports.

SUGGESTED RESEARCH TASKS

Some of our suggested tasks for research can be accomplished by interviews and conversations, or by using pictures, records, and tapes rather than printed materials. This kind of research work can be done by primary-level children or those with limited reading skills. For these children, the resulting information and the conclusions drawn can be dictated to the teacher, a classroom aide, or even to a child with more advanced skills. Or they can simply be the basis for a group discussion to follow the research. You should select from the suggested tasks those ideas that meet some apparent need in your class. Hopefully, you will find many that will be useful.

Family and Neighborhood Research

What responsibilities do you have in your home? How are your responsibilities different from those of other members of your family?

A child who is interested can draw his "family tree," with his or her name on the main trunk, and parents' names on the two main branches that form a V from the trunk. These branches can be continued as far back as parents, grandparents, and other relatives can help with information.

Let a group of children collect information about the national origins of their own and their classmates' grandparents. Explain to them how to make a pictograph using their data. There are many other social studies-oriented graphs that can be made as a result of research by the children, for example: parents' jobs, number of children in each family, favorite foods of foreign origin.

What neighborhood facilities help people communicate with each other? What neighborhood facilities serve the neighborhood but are controlled in some central place?

In the primary grades, work with small groups in developing experience charts about their neighborhood—kinds of homes, transportation facilities, churches and synagogues, schools, streets, highways, friends and neighbors, community helpers. Each child may choose to illustrate some part of the chart, perhaps the part he contributed from his investigations. You can even get upper-grade children to conduct this kind of experience with primary children, and both gain from it.

Community Research

What services does your community supply for its residents? What are the kinds of services supplied by the United States Postal Service? What is meant by Rural Free Delivery, Parcel Post, and Air Mail?

Keep a local telephone book in your classroom. The yellow pages are an especially useful source of information about the kinds of jobs and services that are available in your community, and the many kinds of products that can be purchased. Children can find out, for example, how many veterinarians there are in your community, how many television repair services, whether there are more doctors or lawyers, what kinds of jobs are unique to your community, some of the services and products that are unfamiliar to the class. What is an actuary? an appraiser? an abattoir? an exterminator? Some children can check the ads for employment agencies to see what kinds of jobs are mentioned as being in demand.

Children can get in touch with local industries to find out what is produced, how the products are made, the source of their raw materials, how and where the products are shipped.

Have the children do some research about planned communities such as Reston, Virginia; Columbia, Maryland; and Tapiola, Finland. Vertical files of the Public Library and copies of the Periodical Index are good reference sources.

What are some of the sounds and smells that can be recognized in your neighborhood? in your community?

Groups of children can interview older people who have lived in your community for a long time—possibly a grandparent or neighbor of someone in the group—with the purpose of finding what life in the community used to be like.

What familiar streets had no houses on them? What factories were not yet built? How many schools were there? What kinds of transportation facilities were there? Were there supermarkets? Where did people buy their food? Were there farms? shopping centers? parks?

Individuals can investigate the complete texts of famous American speeches containing well-known quotations. They can also find out when and where the speeches were delivered, and the events that gave rise to the speeches. Some possible quotations to locate are:

You shall not crucify mankind upon a cross of gold.

William Jennings Bryan

Give me liberty or give me death.

Patrick Henry

. . . that government of the people, by the people, and for the people, shall not perish from the earth.

Abraham Lincoln

The only thing we have to fear is fear itself.

Franklin D. Roosevelt

Ask not what your country can do for you.

John F. Kennedy

I have a dream.

Martin Luther King

Some children can use the text of the United States Constitution to find answers to questions that you may give them.
What are the age requirements for President? for Senator? for Representative? In what ways can the Constitution be amended? How can the President be impeached?
Children can also investigate why Thomas Jefferson did not sign the Constitution.

A research venture could be suggested for someone who is interested in the history of money in the United States. It might be called "From Wampum to Credit Cards."

After some research into the operation of the United States Postal Service, the children can develop a class post office. They can design their own stamps, accept and sort and deliver mail addressed to classmates, even plan a Special Delivery service. A dish drainer makes an acceptable sorter. If the operation is expanded into a post office for the whole school, boxes or cubbyholes can be arranged to hold the mail for each class.

Children interested in transportation can do research on related subjects, and can then meet as a group to discuss their findings. Some possible subjects are biographies of the Wright brothers, Charles Lindbergh, or Henry Ford; the history of jet travel; some safety devices for automobile travel; the dirigible and the balloon.

Children can find out what American regional foods are made of. Hush puppies, apple pan dowdy, hominy grits, collards, johnny cake, chitlins, scrapple, Boston beans, Boston and Manhattan clam chowders, seven sweets and seven sours, bouillabaise, and corn pone are only a few such foods. If the ingredients are available, you might get a group to try one of the simpler recipes.

With your class, plan a state luncheon to be prepared and served in school by the children, either for themselves or for their parents. The only requirement for food products to be used is that they be grown, processed or both in your state. This will take independent planning by several committees: the "what to serve" committee; the "how much do we need" committee (these are the math experts); the preparation committee; the serving committee; and, of course, the clean-up committee.
   Some cautions:
      • Be liberal about such accessory items as condiments, and accept a product processed by any company that has a state distribution center printed on the label.

- Caution the children about over- or underestimating the amounts of food needed. This is a good opportunity to talk about wastefulness.
- An extra adult will be necessary, especially if your cooking facilities are a distance from your classroom. An electric plate is useful.
- Try to maintain a reasonably balanced menu, since there is a built-in health lesson involved here.

International Research

Simple foods from several areas of the world can be prepared and eaten by the children. This activity provides an excellent opportunity to introduce new tastes and to discourage the "ughs" that often result when foods are new or unusual-seeming. It can be a real experience in understanding and accepting other cultures. You might start with something seasoned with curry, saffron, or sesame. Introduce guacamole (Mexico), yams (West Africa), okra (Sudan), French toast, rice pilaf (Turkey), Japanese tea, taiglach (honey clusters from Israel), fresh coconut, English trifle, fresh figs, peanut soup (Uganda or colonial America), corn bread, ricotta cheese (Italy). Recipes, if needed, are available in many international cookbooks; the Fun and Festivals books (Friendship Press) and the Hi Neighbor books (UNICEF) are also useful. Small groups of children can do the research and planning for individual dishes. Some of the foods require little or no preparation; any necessary preparation should take place in school, with adult assistance and guidance. Occasionally, groups may meet after school in someone's home and bring the food they have prepared to school the next day for explanation and sharing.

Interested children can do research to get accurate information about how traditional costumes from other lands are made. This information can then be applied in dressing dolls or the children themselves. For example, the Indian sari is made of a six-yard piece of material (five yards will do for a child). The child needs an underskirt or petticoat with a tight waistband. Tuck one end of the material into the waistband a little to the right of center. Draw the material counter-clockwise once around the waist, make six even pleats and tuck them into the waistband. The rest of the material goes around the back, under the right arm, then over the left shoulder in front. The sari is worn with a short blouse.

What are the principal teachings of the great religions of the world—Christianity, Judaism, Islam, Buddhism, Hinduism, animism? What, if anything, do they have in common?

Reluctant researchers are sometimes encouraged if you suggest investigation of popular sports in other parts of the world or at other periods in history, for example: bullfighting, soccer, jai alai, boccie, skiing, mountain climbing, cricket, or even medieval sports such as archery or falconry. Some might want to learn about the Olympic games, in ancient times and today.

Insha Allah; Shalom; Namastay; Aloha. Find out what languages are represented in these expressions, what each one means, and what they have in common.

As a result of investigating one of the cooperatives in countries like Finland or Israel, some aspects of cooperation that are close to the children's lives could be explored to help them understand the significance of world cooperation. Starting with a discussion of how families cooperate at home, a group can talk about how cooperation works in the classroom, and how it can be extended and improved. Groups might also want to investigate cooperation between classes in the school, and interschool cooperation in the community.

A very interesting research project can be centered on hats. Investigation will turn up all sorts of hats and headcoverings that relate to a particular place or time. Drawings can accompany this kind of report to make it more explicit. Some ideas that you might suggest are an English bowler, a Turkish fez, an Israeli kibbutz cap or a yarmulka, an Arab gaffiyeh and ghutra, an Indian headdress, a Mexican sombrero, and a western cowboy hat. Select a couple that might be familiar: the children will dig up the others—and more.

During a study of the rice-growing areas of the world, some children can investigate the growing cycle of rice and how it affects family and community life.

General Research in Social Studies

Have each child in a group write a biographical sketch about a famous person, including some false information. Other children can check the information and find out what part of it is erroneous.

Using the table of contents and/or index of any social studies text in your classroom, compile a series of questions for a task card. One basic question could be, "On what pages would you expect to find information about_____?"

Investigate forms of recreation characteristic of an area or historical period being studied. How do they compare with the ways in which we play and relax?

Stamp collecting and mounting should be encouraged, especially since stamps tell a great deal about a country. Some of the things that children can look for in stamps are heroes and heroines, plants and animals, landmarks, and special celebrations.

You can prepare a work sheet for any social studies topic and make copies available to the children. Any researchable question can be included. Emphasize questions that include some problem-solving related to the research questions, for example:

How does the geography of_____affect the daily lives of the people? Why was the_____River so important to life in _____[a historical period]? What effect did the discovery of_____have on subsequent world history? How did_____influence the people of his country?

Many sources of information—books, pamphlets, filmstrips, pictures—should be available in both the classroom and the library or media center. Children can help each other find information, and may solicit help from their parents. Don't rule out parents' assistance in developing research experiences.

A real store can be developed as a group project, selling cookies whose recipes originally come from areas "visited" in your social studies program. The ingredients for the initial batch can be donated by class mothers; later the project may become self-sustaining, or even profit-making. Children can begin to understand the meaning of specialization by comparing the time involved—and the quality of the finished product—in a one-person effort and in a group effort in which each child is assigned a specific task. Children can sign up to serve as sales personnel at given times; records of costs and sales results can be kept by a committee.

Individual children can plan imaginary trips to places included in the social studies program, incorporating as many details as they wish. To start with, the task cards can suggest means of transportation, the possible cost of trips (ask a travel agency), kinds of clothing to take, specific places of interest to visit, questions to ask the people you meet, things to bring home. If a passport is necessary for the trip, children can investigate passport regulations.

Children can collect, mount, and label samples of natural materials like linen, wool, cotton, wood, rubber, and also synthetics, like plastics and all kinds of man-made textile fibers.

Multi-sensory experiences should be provided whenever possible. You can also encourage responses to such questions as:
If you could visit_____[or, if you lived at the time of_____], what unusual things would you be likely to see? What kinds of sounds and smells would there be? How would the foods taste? What things might you like to touch?

If your social studies program for the year covers several communities or countries, or several historical periods, try to develop a continuing chart that will help the children see differences and similarities at a glance. Block off a large sheet of paper (18" x 24" or larger) with the places or periods listed down the side, and "ways of living" (homes, religion, clothing, recreation, food, occupations, education) across the top. As individual children find information the data can be entered where it belongs. When the chart is completed, comparisons can easily be made.

Reluctant students might be encouraged to do some research about dances of other peoples, for example: the flamenco, the hornpipe, the Highland fling, the hora, and the tarantella. They might also be interested in changes in American dance patterns, from the early square dance to the cakewalk, the two-step, the waltz, the foxtrot, the jitterbug, the twist, and beyond. Some could work in pairs or small groups to demonstrate various dances, and even instruct others who are interested. Your physical education specialist may have information about dance styles and might be a helpful resource person. This kind of research project represents highly specialized interests, and is popular and rewarding if you make the effort to provide the necessary information and material.

map study skills

The introduction of map use should stem from some need or interest expressed by the children. Like other activities, it is more meaningful for the children when it is an outgrowth of a current activity or experience, rather than an isolated unit on map skills. For example, if your primary-level social studies program emphasizes families and communities, you can encourage study involving maps of the classroom, school neighborhood, and community, beginning with the areas closest to the children's experience, and building from there.

Many kinds of maps should be available in the open classroom. You, of course, are best able to judge which kinds you need, according to the ability range of your class and the possible ramifications of your social studies program. Here are some possibilities: globes with up-to-date information; simple outline maps; local maps showing community details; political maps; physical maps; relief maps; maps showing distribution of population, wealth, na-

tural resources, products, races, religions, or languages; historical
maps showing the expansion of cultures and governments over a
period of time; transportation route maps; weather maps.

When you buy commercial maps and globes for use in your class
get those that are simple and uncluttered. This is especially important in an open classroom, because so much of the work is done
independently. Without adult help, many very detailed maps are
confusing and frustrating. If you have a space problem—as many
open classrooms do—use flat paper maps instead of the rollup
variety, so they can be folded and stored easily.

There is an endless variety of exercises and activities to develop
for either individual or small-group involvement. You can select
those that best serve your classroom purposes. Some activities, like
the drawing of large maps on the wall of the room or on the
playground, may even involve the whole class, at different times
and in various phases of the activity.

SUGGESTED MAP SKILL ACTIVITIES

A very simple introduction to the concept of scale drawing can be
done by letting a group of children measure desks or table tops
with a piece of string, then folding the string in half and in half
again until the string length fits on a specific piece of paper. You
can help primary children understand the need for scale drawing
by indicating the size of the paper that would be needed to draw a
life-size picture of the classroom or playground. They can also
understand scale drawing better after tracing each other on large
sheets of wrapping paper on the floor, and then trying to draw the
same person on a regular-size piece of drawing paper. This kind of
activity often starts with just two children and attracts more as it
progresses.

The teaching of direction has possibilities in an open classroom.
The technique of labeling classroom walls with their true direc-

tions has been used by many teachers and is useful for orienting children in a familiar environment. The use of a compass to establish direction is another simple activity, and may lead to scientific investigation about how a compass works or even to making a simple compass. This can be done by resting a magnetized steel needle on a cork that is floating on a dish of water. Games of direction-finding are simple to invent. Groups of children can play Simon Says, using directions: Simon says, "Face east"; "Face north"; Simon says, "Face southwest." Groups that feel they are sufficiently oriented in the classroom can take Simon Says into the playground or the all-purpose room for further reinforcement of these skills. A group of children can play a game of "I'm thinking of . . . ," using directions: "I'm thinking of something in the northeastern part of the room." Additional clues about the size, shape, or use, of the item can be given, and the first person to guess then tells what he's "thinking of" and where in the room it is. A variation is to have one child develop a set of direction clues for a Treasure Hunt: for example, start at the door, walk three paces north and five paces west to find something that holds papers together (a paper clip), then go two paces south and four paces east to find something sweet (a candy).

A small group of children can construct a model of your school and its immediate environs. From this, they can draw a map, using symbols for houses, trees, churches, and so on. They can also become acquainted with the idea of a key or legend by writing explanations of the symbols in the corner of the map. This idea can be expanded into a task involving the construction of a whole community, with civic buildings, parks, bridges, and roads. A map of this model can be drawn, using additional symbols for the key or legend to reinforce this skill.

Road maps provide a readily available source for many tasks. Location skills, marking routes, estimating and accurately calculating distances, and reading keys or legends are some of the many uses for road maps. There are also some interesting and provocative problem-solving situations that can be developed. For example, one possible task that utilizes a local road map is to trace a route that a friend from a nearby community might take to visit your school. The children can find the shortest route, or the least expensive route if there are toll roads in the vicinity. Road maps covering several states are available. Older children can plot a route to a popular tourist area that is separated from your community by other states, for example: a New Jersey shore resort from Ohio; a Maine fishing community from Connecticut; or southwestern Indian reservations from Oregon. Math skills can be reinforced by posing such questions as:

If you travelled about 400 miles a day, how long would it take to get to_____? Where on your route could you stop each day? How many miles an hour would you have to average if you wanted to cover 400 miles in eight hours of driving a day?

The opaque projector is a very useful piece of equipment for map study. You can cover a part of your wall or bulletin board with large sheets of paper, project any map to a size to fit the given area, and have the children trace the outline and the political subdivisions. A large map like this can be used to place points of interest, pictures or samples of products, and geographic aspects. If you have cork bulletin boards, the children can follow the outline of any projection with straight pins, and then put wool or yarn outside the pins to mark the outline. If your walls are cement blocks, groups of children can paint a world map permanently on one wall to use for ready reference, or paint one on a wall in the hallway for other classes to use and enjoy.

If you can get the clear acetate film that is used for transparencies, and the colored film that can be cut and stuck to the clear film, a group of children can make map transparencies for use in an overhead projector. Commercially made transparencies, with overlays, are more accurate, of course, but they are expensive, and lack the dimension of personal involvement for the children. They should be available in media or audiovisual centers when accuracy is essential.

A simple map exercise can be done by a small group of children who visit a local supermarket under adult supervision. They can map the arrangement of the aisles and label the products available in each area of the store. While they are there, they might be encouraged to look for food that is grown or processed in a place they have learned about in school.

Maps of all kinds can be mounted on masonite or plywood and cut on political boundaries with a jigsaw, making excellent puzzles.

A cartographer or a representative of a commercial map company is an excellent resource person to speak to a group of older children who exhibit a particular interest or capacity in this field.

Making relief maps of clay, papier mâché, sawdust and glue, or other media can be a very rewarding experience for children. A sand table is also useful. Even very young children can shape the contours of the school environs to demonstrate varying altitudes. If there is a relatively high spot near your school, consider a trip to that spot with a group of children to help them visualize local topography.

If the blueprints of your school building are available, they can be a valuable source of experience with the many skills involved in map making. Even small children can relate to this "picture" of a familiar place, and begin to understand scale and spatial relationships. Older children can duplicate certain aspects of the blue-prints, scaling them down to a smaller size.

To draw a very large map on a floor or a section of your school playground, trace the map you want to reproduce on a sheet of graph paper; use paper with ½" (or larger) squares. Number each square. Mark with erasable chalk the floor or ground you intend to cover with the same number of squares that the map covers on the graph paper. Number these larger squares—which should measure about six inches—the same way you numbered the graph paper squares. Then each child who wishes to participate can select certain squares on the larger surface. Each section of the map should be drawn with chalk before being marked in paint or some other permanent medium. When all squares are complete, chalk markings that have not been covered can be erased.

language arts and communications skills

There are innumerable ways in which the social studies program in your open classroom overlaps language arts, with or without a deliberate effort on your part. Much of the success of an open classroom social studies program is directly related to the communications skills developed by the children and encouraged by you. Even those tasks performed by individual children gain deeper significance when expressed in speech or writing and discussed with peers. Both children who tend to be withdrawn and those who are outgoing need vehicles through which to express themselves.

COMMUNICATIONS MEDIA

Several activities can be planned to illustrate the general statement that all people need some form of communication. You can find pictures of the sign language used by deaf mutes, and individual children can have a satisfying experience trying to learn this sign language. It is sometimes necessary or desirable for people to communicate with each other in a way that is understood only by them. Children can devise their own hand signals or codes to exemplify this. Breaking a code is a challenging task, and one that requires patience and concentration. You can help with clues about frequently used letters and words. Children who tend to be nonverbal often find code-constructing and code-breaking rewarding. Children can develop a beneficial relationship with each other by working together on a code, as a group, and then using their code to communicate with each other. The resulting camaraderie can promote verbal relationships.

Some children may want to learn the Morse code used in telegraphy, or the semaphore code, to expand their understanding of the many possible methods of communication.

To further elaborate on the importance of all forms of communication, you might suggest various tasks involving research into widely used communications media—radio, television, telephone, telegraph, and satellites, for example: the stories of how each of these communications was started; a simple explanation of how each one works, including pictures and charts; stories speculating about "How My Life Would Be Without _____ [Radio, Television, etc.]"; visits to local radio or television stations, telephone offices, and telegraph offices; three-dimensional models of a telephone, a telegraph key, or a communications satellite (Telstar, Echo, Relay).

POETRY WRITING AND SOCIAL STUDIES

Social studies can provide a great deal of stimulation for your class poets. While children should be given free rein for poetic expression of all kinds, some respond more readily if a stylized form of poetry is suggested to them. So, for those who need or want some inspiration, you could explain some unrhymed verse forms.

- Haiku, a Japanese poetry form of 17 syllables, usually in three lines of five, seven, and five syllables respectively. For example:

Hopping kangaroos,
Koalas and bandicoots,
Live in Australia.

- Cinquains can consist of five lines of two, four, six, eight, and two syllables respectively. For example:

Pueblos—
Zuñi, Hopi,
Southwest Indian tribes.
Make homes of adobe and stone.
Peaceful.

Cinquains can also consist of five one-, two-, three-, four-, and one-word lines respectively. For example:

Africa—
Many countries,
All seeking freedom.
Interesting, exciting, searching, colorful,
Hopeful.

The writing of limericks can be introduced as a suggested task while studying about England, since England's Edward Lear was well known for his limericks. Limericks are a simple verse form, and an excellent vehicle for producing the nonsense verses so dear to children. You can read one or two of Lear's limericks to the groups of prospective poets, to give them a pattern to follow.

Social Studies Riddles

Children can make up riddles, the answers to which are covered in the social studies program. Give them an example for the starter and they'll do the rest.

"I was a black woman. I escaped from slavery in 1849, and then helped more than 300 slaves escape to the North through the Underground Railroad. Who am I? *Harriet Tubman.* Or, "I live in a city that has places called Piccadilly Circus, Downing Street, Trafalgar Square, and Threadneedle Street. Where do I live?" *London.*

DRAMATIC PLAY

In addition to role-playing, the children can plan more organized dramatic play. They can, for example, create a setting for an early pioneer home, a typical village home in a foreign country, or a local supermarket or hospital. Scripts can be simple or detailed, as their interests dictate. Older children can work out a mock United Nations meeting or an election campaign meeting. Your class treasure chest can be a source of props and costumes. If many cultural backgrounds are represented in your school, children can represent their own ethnic or religious groups by acting out typical holiday celebrations. This kind of activity can help to encourage mutual respect and understanding among children of diverse groups.

A group of children can plan and conduct a mock political convention—an especially appropriate activity when the actual conventions are taking place and are being covered by the mass media. The ramifications of this kind of activity are almost endless—writing and delivering nominating, seconding, and acceptance speeches, lettering signs for state delegations, and tallying votes for candidates are a few to begin with. Other children can act as radio and television reporters. This project could conceivably involve almost all phases of your class program—language arts, creative arts, and math, as well as the concomitant social studies learnings—and could become a whole-class activity.

Pantomime

Pantomime can be a medium of expression for some of your less verbal students. It can be developed simply and spontaneously, or planned with care. Some possibilities: lumberjacks sawing down a giant tree; farmers milking cows, feeding livestock, pitching hay; community helpers doing their jobs—firemen putting out fires, policemen directing traffic, sanitation men collecting garbage, mailmen delivering mail; the observance of various customs in places being studied—breaking a piñata in Mexico or Central America, flying kites in Thailand, mounting a camel in Saudi Arabia or North Africa, wrapping a sari on an Indian woman, using castanets in Spain. Children can work out these pantomimes individually or in pairs and then present them for the whole class to try to guess what they represent.

SOCIAL STUDIES GAMES

Commercial social studies-oriented simulation games like Monopoly, Ghetto, and Rescue in Space are fun and informative. There are some flash-card type games called Teach Me About the United States and Teach Me About the President which are also useful. Investigate the toy departments of your local stores for many others. You can also make your own games, using familiar strategies, and local or program-oriented situations.

Try a game of Instant Word Reaction with a group of children. Mention a place, a person, an event—anything related in some way to your social studies program. The children are to answer with one word that they think of instantly. For example, "New York" may bring forth "big," "noisy," or "interesting"; "Civil War" may produce "slaves" or "Lincoln"; "Bangkok" may result in "canals" or "monks." After the children become familiar with the game, they can conduct it themselves, either as a round-robin or with one of the children as the leader. These instant reactions from the children can provide some insights into individual children's values and maturity levels—information that can be useful to the classroom teacher in evaluation procedures.

FOREIGN LANGUAGE EXPERIENCES

If you do not have foreign language training or experience, try to get someone to introduce some of your interested children to the language of a country that they are now studying. Children in the class who speak any of these languages can instruct small groups of their classmates. Just listening to the sound of the language and learning a few simple words is a worthwhile experience.

SOCIAL STUDIES VOCABULARY

Develop a vocabulary list of words related to your social studies program, adding to lists and changing them as emphases change. Keep the list in some conspicuous place so that the children can refer to it easily. General words—"community," "country," "continent," "minority," "government"—that recur frequently in the program can remain posted throughout the year. Be sure to include foreign words that are in common American usage.

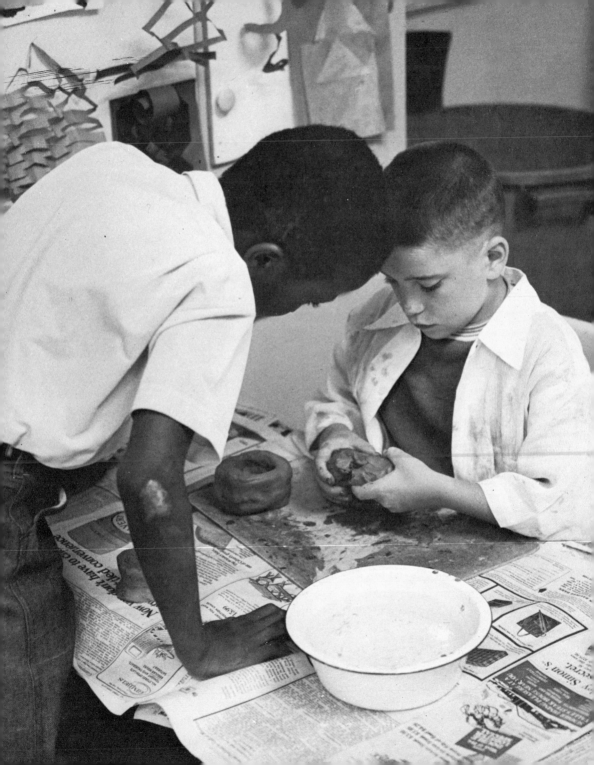

art cart activities

Social studies in an open classroom lends itself to innumerable creative activities centered around your Art Cart, or whatever you may decide to call the interest center where you collect art materials and ideas. Self-portraits, family portraits, pictures of houses in the community, pictures of various kinds of transportation, pictures of people and places studied in school—all these are undoubtedly included in your day-to-day activities, and are, of course, social studies oriented. The most productive activities are those suggested and implemented by the children, but even these may be based upon some hints or possibilities that you have offered. Often, just having materials available encourages the children to develop plans for many imaginative art ventures.

We will try to spell out a few ideas that you may adapt to your own situation. If you keep your Art Cart stocked with any materials and supplies that seem appropriate for your social studies program, probably your only problem will be to find time and space

57

for all the children who would like to work with these materials. As new materials and ideas become available, your enthusiasm in presenting them to the children will be a key factor in inspiring their interest and in channeling their creativity into these undertakings.

Primary-grade children can use cardboard cartons and boxes to construct mail boxes, street signs, fire alarm boxes, and traffic lights. In follow-up group discussions each child can be responsible for explaining his project and how it is useful in the community.

Children can make simple puppets from paper bags, papier mâché, sacks stuffed with cotton or cloth, or two-dimensional figures pasted to tongue depressors. These and other improvisations can be used for all sorts of dramatizations: an historic event; a situation in the life of a family in the United States (miners, migrant workers, farmers, city dwellers, ranchers); or a traditional celebration in some other area of the world. One group of children can write the script and another group can make the puppets and operate them. Children who are subject to stage fright sometimes open up when involved with puppets, especially those that they have made themselves and can identify with.

Use cut paper or mosaic tiles to make mosaics such as those used in murals and other decorations in Mexico, Italy, and London, for example. Mosaics were also used in ancient Greece and Rome, as well as in early Egypt, and could relate to studies of these areas.

Children can make bookmarks illustrating various activities, landmarks, or physical features of places and times that they study about: Big Ben in London; the mountains of Switzerland; the "umbrella" hats and the parasols of Thailand; the covered wagons of the early American pioneers; Indian headdresses; a kangaroo or koala from Australia.

If some children work more successfully on larger surfaces, the same kinds of pictures can be done as posters instead of bookmarks. If you use a task card for this activity, the card might suggest a "bookmark or poster with a picture of something that comes to mind when you think of _____ ." This will leave the principal initiative with the child. Encourage the children to do some research before beginning these pictures so that details will be accurate. This will help the children to see that this is a social studies activity as well as an art venture.

Murals and friezes about life in the United States, in other countries, or at other times in history, can be rewarding group experiences. The overall plan can be discussed by the group that selects a particular subject; then specific jobs can be assigned by the group to each of its members. Some children may draw intricate details of the mural; others can fill in background areas, such as sky, sand, or water. Each child in the group can work at his interest and at his ability level, and since the finished product belongs to the group, each child can share in the success of the endeavor. Incidentally, if large sheets of paper are not readily available, old window shades are excellent for this project.

If you make available an assortment of the following materials, some of the children can make musical instruments similar to those used by many people of the world. Coffee cans, old inner tubes, and rubber cement can be used to make drums. Dried gourds, papier mâché on old electric bulbs, or paper cups with pebbles in them are excellent maracas. Plastic straws or bamboo sticks can make usable wind instruments. Flat stones, tongue depressors, and sandpaper-covered wooden blocks can make simple percussion instruments. Many other possibilities will occur to you and to the children once a venture like this is started.

Making masks from heavy paper or papier mâché can be rewarding, and related to many different aspects of social studies. The colorful masks of the tribes of western and central Africa, the masks and totems of the Pacific Northwest Indians, and the gold and turquoise masks worn by the Aztecs are just a few possibilities. Chinese dance and drama use interesting masks, and the masks of the ancient Greek and Roman theatre might be pertinent to your program. If masks really catch on in your class, children might try making surgeon's masks, catcher's masks, and even gas masks.

Further investigation into the meaning of totems might inspire some children to draw or construct totems for their families, representing animate objects that they hold in esteem. A group might even want to design a totem for the class, using its pet fish, hamster, or gerbils as a symbol of the group's unity.

Suggest that children use large sheets of paper to trace each other lying on the floor. On these life-size figures, they can draw children's clothing of other countries or historical periods. These make good bulletin board displays if there is enough room.

For primary children, you can make a picture of numbered dots to follow in sequence to form the outline of a product, familiar building or other landmark, community helper, or even a community or state map. When completed, these outlines can be appropriately colored, if the children wish.

Individuals or groups can design original stamps representing some facet of life in a country being investigated—its history, an industry, a well-known place, a plant or animal, a famous person, a holiday or special celebration.

Encourage children to try to use imaginative, creative lettering for reports done in conjunction with any phase of the social studies program. For example, SWITZERLAND can be printed in many different sizes of letters, so that the word looks like a series of mountain peaks. FINLAND can have some of the letters decorated as trees to represent the forests. A report on an OASIS in the desert could use the O as the sun and the I as the trunk of a palm tree. ISRAEL could be lettered, using the I as the center of a menorah (seven-branched candlestick) and the A as half of the Star of David. One simple idea given to a group of budding artists will surely bring fantastic results.

A simple but rewarding task is to draw and color the flags of countries that are being studied. Be sure that research precedes this project to ensure its accuracy.

problem-solving

Problem-solving techniques are among the most significant points of method shared by social studies and open classroom programs. These techniques and their implementation are consequently central to all phases of your open classroom social studies program. Searching for and finding answers to all kinds of problems are basic procedures. Since most problems do not have easy answers, making mistakes is an inherent aspect of these activities. In an open classroom, we more readily accept mistakes as part of the problem-solving process. It may be that some problems will not really be solved, but the process is no less important in these situations.

The enriched environment of the open classroom is ideal for the development and possible solution of all kinds of problems. Without suggestions from you, many problem-solving situations result simply from the social atmosphere in the room and the presence of many curiosity-stimulating materials. Problem-solving should emphasize the fact that learning is not a teacher-centered operation, but the result of searching for answers from many sources, especially personal experiences.

Questions and problem-solving situations that you suggest should be directed toward understanding ideas and generalizations, not toward the memorization of facts. As people and events are discussed in groups or considered in individual inquiries, the children's optional tasks should stress the exploration of why the events took place and how conditions and events affect people. In short, questions should be meaningful, emphasizing how and why, instead of what and when.

Since a major goal of your program will be the development of respect for other people and their ways of life, the answers to the questions of why people live and act as they do should be explored. Questions should investigate the ways in which people's lives are affected by climate, land forms, and natural resources, as well as by their history and background. Only by this kind of exploring can children begin to understand and accept differences, without judging whether a different way of life is better or worse than theirs.

Depending upon the needs of your class and the requirements of your social studies program, you can select some of the following questions to be put on task cards for individual exploration, or as a basis for discussion with a small group of interested children. If these discussions arouse interest, other children may get involved, some as listeners, some as active participants. In some instances, you may want to suggest that two or more children who have discovered answers to one of these questions could get together to discuss their conclusions. In this way, the interaction may develop a new, and different, group solution to the problem. This will help in the realization that these problems do not have one "right" answer.

Many of the suggested problem-solving tasks can be resolved through **role-playing,** a technique involving the acting out of a problem, instead of talking or writing about it. Role-playing, or **sociodrama,** is unrehearsed. For any given problem, children select roles to play and spontaneously act out the problem situation. The values of role-playing as a problem-solving technique are varied: it stimulates active participation in the solution of the problem; it encourages communication of ideas; it develops sensitivity to and understanding of feelings and values. In social studies it is particularly valuable in helping children explore the reasons for certain living patterns and possible solutions for social problems. In your open classroom, groups of children can present role-playing situations to the whole class, and then conduct follow-up discussions as "experts."

SUGGESTED PROBLEM-SOLVING TASKS

Some of the following tasks can be adapted to any grade or any program. Others meet more specific needs. Most are merely the basis on which you as a creative teacher can begin to develop your own ideas.

Individual and Family Problem Situations

What basic needs do all people have, wherever they may live?

What are some of the things that most parents want for their children? Explain why they might want each of the things you mention.

How do you select your friends in school? in your neighborhood?

How do most people select their jobs? What are some of the things you would consider before choosing a job?

What could you do to make yourself understood by a classmate or a neighbor who could not speak or understand English or any other language that you speak or understand?

What are some of the reasons that people move from one home to another?

Try an experiment in privilege and prejudice. With the cooperation of the class, select a group of children with one or more brothers and sisters, and another group that has no siblings. (You can have groups of blondes and brunettes, or any other grouping that occurs to you.) First let both groups discuss the reasons for prejudice and some of its manifestations. The smaller group is the "minority" for your experiment. Have both groups role-play the situation for part of a day. The "majority" group thinks of certain "rights" and privileges to demand—play periods, more comfortable seats, use of the drinking fountain, choice of supplies and equipment. You might even provide cookies to the "privileged" group. After role-playing this minority–majority situation, both groups together can discuss how this experiment shows the development of privileged groups, and the resulting minority problems. With careful guidance, the children can relate this to a neighborhood or community situation with which they are familiar. The final question for the group could be, "Since our local problem has no more basis in fact than our classroom experiment did, what can we do about solving it?"

A group of children whose family situation includes some concern about grandparents might meet to discuss their feelings about whether grandparents should live alone or with their families. Possibly your social studies program includes the study of a culture where the family unit always includes grandparents. Pros and cons of these situations can be discussed, but no group conclusion should be expected.

What are some of the important problems facing our community?
Unemployment? Crowded schools? Pollution? Water shortage?
Slums? Traffic congestion? What solutions do you suggest?

What things would you like to have changed in your community?
Explain the reason for each change and your suggestions for possible improvements. Illustrate your suggestions if you think that
pictures, maps, or charts would be helpful for explanations.

A group of children might write to the local governing body to
explain their joint ideas about changes in the community. If a visit
can be arranged, it would be even more meaningful.

Why do people move from large cities to smaller communities?
Why do they move from smaller communities to large cities?

Why do some communities have apartment houses while others
do not?

What places are there in your local community where people can
learn, other than schools?
A group meeting to discuss their individual findings may determine that people can learn in almost any place.

Using road maps of your local area, have groups of interested
students figure out what roads could be used to get from a nearby
community to your community if, for example, a particular bridge
washed out, a particular portion of a main road was being
resurfaced, or a broken water main had caused a cave-in that closed
the usual way of traveling between the two communities.

Suggest that some children trace the outline of one of their hands on a large piece of paper, and then write on each "finger" one of the major services that a community should offer its people—schools, fire and police, health services, parks and recreation. It's a community "helping hand."

If the local community were struck by a major catastrophe, like an earthquake, a tornado, a major fire, or a flood, what would be the order of priorities for getting back to normal? Food? Water? Housing? Clothing? Medicine? Explain the reasons for the order you selected. After the emergency needs have been met, what plans must be made for the future? What priority should be given to the rebuilding of schools, industries, transportation, or communications? Explain your answers.

Think about an imaginary community that you would consider an almost perfect place to live.

What kind of climate would it have?
What kinds of food would the people eat?
How would they dress?
What kinds of transportation would the people use?
What games would they play?
What natural resources would there be?
What industries would there be?
What animals and plants would live there?
What kind of government would there be?
Explain each one of your choices. Draw a map and some pictures of your community and give it an appropriate name.

United States Problem Situations

Two groups, role-playing as colonists after the Revolutionary War, can debate the question: Should the thirteen colonies become one nation, or exist as thirteen independent states?

Why does the school calendar in most public schools of the United States include a two-month vacation in the months of July and August?

Suggest investigation into our early agrarian society. Individual children can consider the advantages and problems involved in the system. Children of schoolteachers may find this an especially interesting topic. A group can meet after independent investigations and discuss their findings. They can also interview classmates about the twelve-month school year, and report general reactions to the class. They may also want to ask members of the school staff about their thoughts in this matter.

Do you agree that education in the United States must always be free and compulsory? Why or why not?

Why is radio used so widely in spite of the popularity of television? If you were in charge of advertising for a large company, what medium would you use most—radio, television, newspaper advertising, magazine advertising, or direct mail? Explain your answer.

What do you consider some of the causes of poverty? What do you think are some of the possible solutions?

Let a group try to figure out how they would budget a specific salary for a family of six for a year. How much would they plan for housing? food? clothing? Discuss with the group, "What can we do about poverty in the United States?" Try to encourage suggestions for many alternative solutions, and discuss the pros and cons of each, for example: increased welfare aid from the government; more jobs in government and private industry; better educational opportunities and more widely available vocational training; better use of natural resources.

International Problem Situations

How are the lives of the people in_____[name of particular country or area of a country] affected by climatic conditions such as temperature, seasonal winds (hurricanes, tornadoes, monsoons), the amount and kind of precipitation? How are the lives of the people affected by geographic features such as rivers, mountains, oceans, volcanoes, lakes, forests, or a natural seaport? Which of these things has affected life in your local community? How?

How do people adapt to their environment? How do things like homes, food, clothing, recreation vary according to environment?

How do people change their environment to meet their needs?

Encourage free-flowing, open-ended discussions or written statements on "How I Feel About _____ [a place, person, event]."

Let children, either individually or in small groups, examine untitled pictures of locations studied during the year. Some commercial study prints are available, and travel posters or pictures from travel agencies may also be used. Try to get pictures that give some clues to answering the following questions and others.

> How might people earn a living in this place? Why?
> What kind of clothing might they wear? Why?
> What kind of food might they eat? Why?
> What might they do for recreation? Why?

Attach a United States or foreign coin to a task card, and ask on the card:

If you were an archaeologist and you uncovered this coin in your digging, what might you conclude about the culture of the people who lived at the time the coin was used?

You can, if you wish, make suggestions, such as "What about the metal used? the picture on the coin? the writing on the coin?"

General Problem Situations

Use accounts of the same event in two or more daily newspapers to compare the details. Why are these "facts" often different?

Prepare a set of cards, each one with the name of an important person or a simple explanation of an important event on it. Shuffle the cards and distribute them equally to children in the group. The children are to arrange themselves in the correct order in a sort of living time line. To make these cards, be sure to select people and events whose sequence is significant in the procession of an historical period, rather than tenuously related people and events whose dates must be memorized.

Mail order catalogues from several companies can be used to develop consumer awareness in your students. Tasks can be set up asking for comparative prices for the same article from different companies. Questions to consider could be:
Does the description of the item that is more expensive indicate in some way that it is better than the cheaper item? If not, how can you account for the difference in prices? In your local community, are there stores where similar items can be purchased for less money than in other stores? Why is this? Why do people shop in stores that charge more?

Let children select from a list of "what if" questions and speculate about possible answers. They can think about these possibilities and write out answers individually, then meet in a group to compare conclusions. Here are some examples.

What if the United States had not made the Louisiana Purchase in 1803?

What if Alaska and Hawaii had not become states?

What if the Indians had conquered the white settlers and had been able to retain their territory?

What if the South had won the Civil War?

What if the United States had not entered World War II?

What if Thomas Edison had never lived?

expanding horizons

Here are a few aspects of a social studies program which we ourselves have explored in greater depth. We present them as ideas that have been interesting and significant enough to merit additional attention. They may not necessarily meet your particular class needs, but they do indicate ways in which your social studies program can be highlighted.

CURRENT EVENTS ACTIVITIES

Encourage the discussion of events and issues, including controversial ones such as local strikes and elections. Get at least one daily newspaper and one weekly newsmagazine in your classroom, and use weekly news publications designed for use in schools, the Scholastic magazines and Weekly Reader, for example, as a basis for group discussions. Encourage the children to watch or listen to regular news programs on television or radio; in addition, the news programs geared to school children on some educational stations can be brought to their attention. Watch for important television news documentaries that might interest your children. Remind them of the date, time, and subject, and plan a small group discussion with those children who watch the program.

Small groups can discuss current events at more or less regular intervals or for several days in a row if a situation is particularly interesting. You should expect to moderate at least the first few meetings. A radio or television news program during class time might start a discussion. You may act as moderator for these, with such remarks as "There are some people who think that . . .," but the discussions should be free and open. Try to get children to see the distinction between fact and opinion.

Children may want to become "experts" on a particular subject. Some may specialize in local news, others in national or international items. Some may want to specialize in a particular phase of current events, following the progress of one situation day by day and collecting clippings for a poster or scrap book. Interesting projects might include a Presidential trip, an election campaign, the progress of a favorite sports team, or a major disaster such as a hurricane or a volcanic eruption. The latter could lead to scientific investigations of causes, as well as social studies-based research. Children may become regional experts, developing year-long interests in Asian or African affairs, for example. You might also have a group investigate the same news item as it appears in different media—newspapers, magazines, radio, and television. Along similar lines, individual children can collect reports from two or more newspapers about the same news event, and read them to a group. The group can then discuss differences in reporting and select the account they think most accurate or most interesting. A group of children interested in news reporting could prepare a news report to be announced over the school's public address system, or typed and duplicated for distribution to other classes. This can be a daily or a weekly assignment, according to their preference.

Using a large world map, post clippings about important current events around the map, and then connect the clippings to their geographical locations with yarn or string. If you mount the map on a hallway wall, then other classes can cooperate in the effort and share its lessons.

Children with artistic interests can draw cartoons related to current events; others may want to collect political cartoons from newspapers and magazines and write their explanations of what the cartoonist means. You can cut out and mount simple cartoons from newspapers and magazines, and attach a task card asking such questions as:
What message does this cartoon express? Who are the people in this cartoon? Do you agree with the message?
You will have to be selective about the cartoons you present, gauging your selections by the maturity of the children and their background in the subject portrayed.

The classified (want ad) section of the newspaper can provide many interesting and informative activities. Questions to be discussed might include:
For what kind of job are there the most vacancies? How do you account for this? How would you find out where to get a used air conditioner? Where would you look to find a lost pet? Are there separate listings for jobs for men and women? Why or why not? How much would it cost to put an ad in this section of the newspaper? Do you think that this kind of advertising is as effective as regular advertising in the newspaper? Why or why not ?

THE USE OF RESOURCE PEOPLE

Here are some suggestions for broadening your program by using resource people from your community or outside it.

Invite people who have visited or lived in areas of the world that are included in your program, or areas where geography or culture are sufficiently similar to those studied that comparisons can be made. Ask these guests to bring pictures, slides, or any realia that they may have gathered.

Try to get experts in fields directly related to your social studies program, for example, a cartographer, a zoo keeper, a museum employee, a newspaper reporter or editor, a foreign cooking expert, a farmer.

Members of the local community governing body or the Board of Education, as well as any other community department or agency, can be interesting guests. They can discuss the work of their particular body and answer questions about local problems.

There are some cautions to exercise when your class invites resource people to visit.

• It is helpful to meet the guest prior to his visit, and make sure that he is aware of the age of your children, of certain basic conditions, such as the kinds of things that might interest them, and the approximate amount of time that can be allotted. If possible, you should preview slides, pictures, or souvenirs so that you can make some prudent suggestions; tourists sometimes bring home endless family photographs that are boring to children.

• Be sure that your guest knows that you have an open classroom, especially if his group will be meeting in the same room as the rest of the class. Prepare him for the possibility—probability,

really—of some sound and movement in the room. If you arrange
for the children to meet with the guest elsewhere in the school, this
problem might be avoided.

• Be sure that the group that is going to talk with the visitor has
had some preparation. It is important not to limit their spontaneity,
but they should discuss, for example, what questions to ask the
visitor. If they plan to take notes about the meeting, they should
have pencil and paper at hand so that the visitor's time is not
wasted. They might even want to arrange to tape the visit in order
to have a permanent record of it.

• The group that meets with a visitor should be responsible for
writing a letter or note thanking him for sharing his experiences
with them.

Using community resource people is slightly different in an open
classroom than in a more traditional setting. In your program,
groups of children may select an area of interest to be heightened
by a discussion with an expert in the field. Consequently, the size
of the group with whom the visitor talks can vary from very small
to the entire class, depending on how many become involved. It is
even possible to invite an individual to speak with one child who
has displayed a genuine interest in the guest's field of expertise.

FIELD TRIPS

Whatever their scope, field trips represent additional life experiences for the class and help children acquire knowledge of the
world around them. The concept of field trips has a much more
varied application in any open classroom than it would in a traditional class. Many activities spill over into the halls, playground,
and other areas of your school environment, and many excursions
outside your own room take on the aspect of a social studies-related "field trip." A child visiting the office or library to interview a
secretary or librarian, a group visiting the boiler room with the

custodian, a group painting a giant map on the playground, or cleaning up the playground as part of their study of ecology—all these come under the heading of field trips for an open classroom.

In addition to daily activities that are an integral part of a social studies program in an open classroom, you can also consider planning more extensive trips, either for small groups or for the whole class. Ideally, other adults will be regular members of your classroom community, so that groups of children can take field trips that serve their particular interests and activity. Short walks around the school environs help primary children learn to identify various street signs, and encourage them to try drawing maps or pictures of the area. If civic elections are held in your school, try to take groups to visit the polls. Trips can be made to historic sites, public buildings, newspaper printing plants, radio and television stations and libraries, among other places. A trip to a nearby cemetery with old headstones can give some clues about the early history of your area.

What was the average age at which people died during a particular era? What does this indicate? What were some of the old family names? Are some of these families still in the community?

A trip around the community with emphasis on geographic features is also a valuable experience. Noting rivers, ponds, hills, and valleys, and drawing conclusions about why certain streets follow geographic contours can be interesting at any grade level. Older children make more sophisticated observations and arrive at more mature conclusions about why the community happens to be located where it is, and how the various sections of the community developed as they did.

Why is the industrial section located where it is? the residential area? the slums? shopping centers?

In preparing for such a trip, you can pose certain questions to the class. Upon return to school, small groups can meet to discuss their observations and arrive together at certain conclusions.

Field trips outside the local community probably should be planned for your whole class, since they may take a full school day and it may be difficult to arrange coverage of two groups for that length of time. Even a whole-class trip to a nearby museum will uncover numerous possibilities for individual children to visit many different kinds of exhibits, depending upon their particular interests. If you find that you cannot build individual activity into the field trip itself, you can serve individual interests by planning small-group discussions as a follow-up to the trip.

ECOLOGY

The study of our environment is really an exercise in reponsibili-ty, since each of us is accountable for the condition of our surroundings and our use of natural resources. In recent years, we have become increasingly aware that our actions are important not only for the future but also for now. Since social studies in the open classroom is concerned primarily with people and their lives, we cannot overstate the importance of ecology and inculcating responsibility for our environment in class study. You may consid-er this part of your science program. Since labels and classifica-tions often overlap, we feel that there is also justification for considering it in the context of a social studies program.

A great deal can be done, individually and in small groups, to encourage your students' active concern with the problems of air and water pollution, excessive litter, noise pollution, and over-population. The need for conservation of all our natural resources will become apparent to the children as they discuss specific prob-lems. There are many tasks that you can suggest for the children, or activities that you can launch with them. Here are a few of our ideas.

Have the class collect glass and aluminum cans and have them brought to local collection centers for recycling.

Have a group compose a list of things that their families can do to ease pollution problems and help conserve resources, for example: don't waste water; use ecologically sound detergents or soap; reuse bags and containers of all kinds; don't litter; use car pools or bicycles and walk whenever possible; buy liquids in returnable bottles; avoid gift wrapping when possible; turn off lights and appliances when not in use. Duplicate these lists and have children take them home to encourage their families' participation.

Write class letters to state and federal legislators asking for stricter anti-pollution laws. Children can write letters to local newspaper editors expressing concern about local environmental problems. The class might write to manufacturers of items like foods and cosmetics, asking for elimination of extra wrappings such as tubes, bottles, or plastic bags in boxes.

If there are industrial plants in your area, get a Ringelmann scale that shows degrees of industrial smoke in the atmosphere. (A science teacher may have one and can explain in simple terms how to use it.)

Cover several pieces of cardboard with oil or petroleum jelly. Hang a few inside the classroom and a few outdoors, and compare results. You can use masking tape with similar results.

Get two small fishbowls; put two goldfish in each. Have the children put a filter in one; they can add a small amount of oil to the other. They can keep a diary of the activity of the fish. As soon as the ones in the "polluted environment" begin to swim a little more slowly (become lethargic), they can be put into the other "pollution-free environment," and the children can observe any change.

Individual children can analyze the immediate neighborhood of
your school in ecological terms. Your suggested task can include
such questions as:
Are there enough trees in our neighborhood to supply beauty and
shade, and prevent soil erosion? Is our neighborhood crowded?
Are there parks and play areas where people have enough open
space for recreation? Do you think the houses are too close
together? Are there many business and industrial buildings in our
neighborhood? Are these buildings ugly, or have some of them
been built to look pleasing and inviting? Do you like our neighborhood? Why or why not? What improvements would you like to see
in our neighborhood? How do you think these improvements
could be made?

The beauty and the ugliness of various aspects of the children's
environment can be the inspiration for some creative writing—either poetry or descriptive prose. You might try to find some poetry
to read to the group to encourage their own attempts. Pictures of
the beauties of nature and some of the ugliness that man has caused
could also serve as inspiration. Children who collect rocks or shells
can use their experience as possible subjects for writing. Encourage
the use of colorful vocabulary by providing dictionaries and
thesauri for the children.

A group can speculate on problems resulting from increasing
population. For example:
How would life change if the population of the local community
doubled? What additional facilities and services would be needed?
How would you feel about such an increase in population?

Individual children can do some research into specific environmental problems: the deadly smog in London in December 1952
and what the Londoners did about it; the problem of rats in Ameri-

can cities; how destructive weeds can be controlled; flash floods —their causes and problems of controlling them; sandstorms on the deserts of the world; DDT and other insecticides—how they destroy plant and animal life; the San Andreas Fault and the problems of earthquakes.

Science-oriented children can investigate the meaning of decibels and how sound is measured. Community governments often have an expert in some department who uses a sound-level meter to test for violations of local codes. Get this equipment demonstrated and discuss the community's regulations about noise.

Committees can investigate various aspects of conservation—water, wildlife, forests, minerals. Information is available from many concerned organizations such as the National Wildlife Federation, the National Audubon Society, and the Sierra Club, as well as from the United States Forest Service and the United States Department of the Interior.

AMERICA'S CULTURAL DIVERSITY

In the course of the school day, most children come into contact with other children from a variety of ethnic backgrounds. Children tend to feel insecure when faced with cultural or racial differences, and it is sometimes this insecurity that breeds prejudice. It is therefore the responsibility of all teachers to help children develop sufficient understanding of these differences to produce a feeling of security in order to avoid stereotyped images and minimize prejudice.

Those who teach social studies in an open classroom have many opportunities for one-to-one and small-group relationships, where inhibitions can be broken down and free and easy discussions can take place. Much of the success in such an effort depends upon the attitudes of the teacher. Some soul-searching and self analysis may be worthwhile. It is fallacious to assume that teachers do not have the prejudices of lay people. It would be more honest to accept the practical truth of our own prejudices, and to try to examine them, investigate the facts, and reevaluate our own positions. Lester Pearson, who won a Nobel prize for his work at the United Nations, said, "All educated and cultured people have a problem in matching what they proclaim with what they actually feel." We must all examine our prejudices candidly. Our responsibility to our students is too great to allow ourselves to indulge in beliefs that are inaccurate, thoughtless, or untrue. When we have developed an awareness of our own attitudes and have made a conscious effort to evaluate them, we are better prepared to share with our students an understanding and acceptance of the diversity of our country. We can then look with them at other people's lives and cultures. Through seeing similarities and differences, the children often see themselves more clearly and appreciate their own uniqueness.

The changing of values in a classroom cannot be accomplished by just talking about them, although discussions and analyses certainly are helpful, and involving children in the process of determining values is the most important step toward their acceptance of these values. A good teacher, through understanding and acceptance of others' traditions, can be both model and inspiration. The teaching of "facts" about ethnic groups is not enough; the important questions of civil rights and social justice, as well as national unity and international peace, must be approached fairly and realistically. A teacher in an open classroom can involve each student in activities at the level of his or her understanding which encourage and deepen positive attitudes toward these questions.

In addition to promoting patriotism for our own country, children of all backgrounds should be encouraged to develop an ethnic identity and a pride in their own ancestry. In the past, the "melting pot" philosophy of assimilation was emphasized. There is now a greater acceptance of the idea that ethnic diversity enriches American culture, and that people should be encouraged to be themselves and retain their ethnic identity. In this way each of the racial and ethnic groups can make a valuable contribution to our society from its own cultural heritage.

By initiating discussions, research, and other activities, you can help the children to understand differences in language, color, religion, and tradition. Classroom interaction can have a profound effect upon students' future attitudes. To a great extent, you, as the classroom teacher, are accountable for the development of these attitudes and actions. Although children should be aware of the contributions of all minorities, the specific emphasis of your program will depend upon your class, school, and community. The fact that certain minorities are not represented in your school population does not mean that their contributions should be omitted from your program, however. It is important that children who have limited opportunities to develop relationships with children representing other minority groups should be made aware of the significant contributions of those groups.

General Sources of Information

Lists of materials about minority groups and human relations are available from many sources. The school or public librarian should be your best guide to these, but here are some possibilities to explore:

The Council on Interracial Books for Children, 9 East 40th St., New York, N.Y. 10016, publishes a quarterly newsletter that includes articles and booklists.

NEA Center for Human Relations, 1201 16th St., N.W., Washington, D.C. 20036, has publications about integrated educational materials, including "An Index to Multi-Ethnic Teaching Materials and Teacher Resources."

NAACP, 1790 Broadway, New York, N.Y. 10019.

National Urban League, Research Department, 55 East 22nd St., New York, N.Y. 10022.

Anti-Defamation League of B'nai Brith, 315 Lexington Ave., New York, N.Y. 10016 (or any regional office).

National Conference of Christians and Jews, Inc., 43 West 57th St., New York, N.Y. 10019.

National Council of Churches, Department of Educational Development, 475 Riverside Dr., New York, N.Y. 10027, has a "Black Heritage Resource Guide" and other human relations material for teachers.

Department of Health, Education and Welfare, Washington, D.C. 20202.

American Federation of Teachers, AFL-CIO, 1012 14th St., N.W., Washington, D.C. 20005.

The Children's Music Center, Inc., 5373 West Pico Blvd., Los Angeles, California 90019, has an annotated catalogue of records and books about all minority groups.

There are innumerable tapes, transparencies, filmstrips, study prints, books, records, and sound films, in addition to kits combining two or more media. It is a good idea to ask your librarian or media specialist to get some of them for you to preview, since many will not meet your needs. Remember, too, that certain kinds of material are more effective than others in an open classroom. Especially useful is material that can be used by individuals or small groups with a minimum of direction from you.

Suggested Tasks

The introduction to the study of minority groups and the problems of human relations can begin with the children's own backgrounds. Most children know something about their own ethnic backgrounds and can share this knowledge with a group. Your participation in such a discussion can be helpful in case inaccuracies need to be corrected, or questions answered. Interested children can use the basic information to carry on further investigations about the contributions made to American culture by people from the countries or ethnic backgrounds represented in the class. Children should be allowed complete freedom to decide whether they prefer to research their own backgrounds or those of their classmates.

Individual children can design all sorts of family trees on which to record the names of their ancestors for as many generations as living family members can recollect. They can use a tree shape with branches and twigs, or make charts; they can use pictures of some of the people; they may be able to find out about relationships between people of different national origin or different religions or different races within their families. Because uncertainty and lack of information make some children uncomfortable about working on a real family tree, some may prefer to fabricate one. A conference can help to clear up some questions about what kind of family tree to work on and how to go about it.

Have all the children find out the national origins of their parents, grandparents, or guardians. A group of interested children can collect this data; they can then locate the countries represented on a world map, and make a graph (bar, pie, or pictograph) that shows the countries represented and the number of family members from each. Children who become interested in this kind of activity can expand it to include interviews with friends and neighbors and graphing their family origins. A discussion may result of the general composition by national origin of the class and how this compares with the neighborhood or the community.

Suggest that individual children or small groups spend some time at a nearby shopping area where many people come and go, near a church on Sunday morning, or outside a movie theater at show break, for example. Have them note the differences they see in the people—hair and skin coloring, types of clothing, estimated age range, and so on. Have them collate their data and try to find out what, if anything, this information tells them about the local community and its surrounding area.

Discuss the meaning of the American Indian prayer that says, "Grant that I may not criticize my neighbor until I have walked a mile in his moccasins." Children can be helped to understand the problems of others by role-playing or by writing a description of how life might be under the following circumstances, what problems might arise, and how the problems might be solved.

Someone in the family marries someone of another religion.
Someone in the family marries someone of another race.
Your parents are migrant workers.
Your parents do not speak English.
Your father loses his job because he cannot speak English well.
Your parents are not American citizens.
Your family has been in the United States for five or six generations.
Your parents do not permit you to play with a friend whose religion is different from yours; with a friend of a different race.

Discuss the true meaning of prejudice, and the difference between harmless prejudices and those that hurt people. For example: Prejudice is a dislike of something or somebody arrived at without knowledge or thought and for no good reason. We may dislike certain kinds of food for no good reason, and that is a prejudice, but it is harmless. But disliking a person for no good reason can hurt that person. How can we show a dislike for something or somebody for a good reason? Would that be considered a prejudice? Why or why not? What makes people develop prejudices? What can we do to avoid becoming prejudiced? How can we stop other people's prejudices?

This kind of question can best be discussed in small groups where there is a greater opportunity for participation; all students should have a chance to be involved in activity of this sort.

Children should be given opportunities to share aspects of their family's culture with a group. Sharing foods, music, dances, language, and holiday customs helps reinforce the concept that we can all enjoy the contributions of different cultural heritages. It also makes unfamiliar things more familiar, and so more enjoyable. Parents and grandparents can be invited to participate in these cultural sharings.

Keep in your classroom for general independent reading some of the numerous good picture books, biographies, and children's novels that have tolerance and race relations as their central themes. As guide and co-learner in your open class, it is important to familiarize yourself with the books your class will be reading, so that you can participate in discussions and help the children compare the life styles and experiences portrayed in the books. You can help them to identify with the concerns and attitudes of the characters in these books. Many useful titles are included in bibliographies from the organizations mentioned earlier. Here are just a few to get your collection started.

Hamilton, Virginia. *The House of Dies Drear*

Jackson, Jesse. *Anchor Man*

Jones, Adrienne. *Sail Calypso!*

Keats, Ezra Jack. *The Snowy Day* and *John Henry*
Lexau, Joan. *Striped Ice Cream*
Mathis, Sharon Bell. *Sidewalk Story*
McGovern, Ann. *Runaway Slave*
Shotwell, Louisa. *Roosevelt Grady*
Stolz, Mary. *A Wonderful, Terrible Time*

BLACK AMERICANS

As an example of the current thrust toward increased under-standing of all races and ethnic backgrounds, we can point to the great amount of material now available relating the historical and cultural contributions of black Americans. *The Negro Almanac* (Harry A. Ploski and Ernest Kaiser, editors. Bellwether Co., 167 East 67th St., New York, N.Y. 10021. 1971) is a comprehensive one-volume reference book for teacher background in this area. There is a thought-provoking article by Dorothy Sterling (*The English Journal*, September 1969) called "What's Black and White and Read All Over?", about the need for a greater understanding of black culture and history.

Suggest some research into the contributions of black American women such as Harriet Tubman, Phillis Wheatley, Rosa Parks, Sojourner Truth, Mary McLeod Bethune, and Marian Anderson. Have individuals investigate stories about black athletes such as Jackie Robinson, Althea Gibson, Wilt Chamberlain, Joe Louis, Jesse Owens, and Willie Mays. Some of your reluctant readers should enjoy this. Children who have shown unusual interest or superior research skills could investigate the contributions of some less well-known distinguished black Americans, for example: Matthew Henson, co-discoverer of the North Pole with Commander Peary; Dr. Charles Drew, organizer of the first blood bank; Jean Baptist Point Du Sable, Chicago's first permanent settler; Frederick M. Jones, who invented the first automatic refrigeration system for trucks; General Benjamin O. Davis, Sr., the first black general in U.S. history. Share with a poetry group poems of Langston Hughes, Paul Laurence Dunbar, Phillis Wheatley, Countee Cullen, Gwendolyn Brooks, James Weldon Johnson. *Famous American Negro Poets* by Charlemae Rollins and *I Am the Darker Brother* edited by Arnold Adoff are two sources.

Some children may be motivated to do in-depth research on the civil rights movement, from the Fourteenth and Fifteenth Amendments to the Supreme Court decisions, and including the best-known past or present leaders of the various groups, for example: Martin Luther King (Southern Christian Leadership Conference); Whitney Young (National Urban League); Malcolm X (Black Muslims); Stokeley Carmichael (Student Non-Violent Coordinating Committee); Roy Wilkins (National Association for the Advancement of Colored People); Floyd McKissick (Congress of Racial Equality). Some research on the problems of American Indians, Mexican-Americans, and Puerto Ricans could be included in this project.

Groups of children can make African and West Indian musical instruments (drums, shakers, and steel pans, for example) and use them to accompany the singing of spirituals, work songs, jazz, or Calypso music.

Copies of *Ebony* will supply interesting pictures and information, and a current events story as reported in *Ebony* can be compared with the reporting of the same event in another newsmagazine.

Children who are just beginning to develop their research skills should have no difficulty finding biographical material about well-known black Americans, including Frederick Douglass, George Washington Carver, Benjamin Banneker, Ralph Bunche, and W.E.B. DuBois.

These black studies tasks are examples of things that you can plan for minority studies as you begin to find material that your children can use. While we see these tasks involving the contributions of minorities as a significant part of a social studies curriculum, we really view the whole approach to cultural diversity as a total human relations concept. It is not just a study of the deprived, the poor, the minorities. Effective human relations cannot be an isolated program in your social studies curriculum. Especially in an open classroom, where mobility and interaction are always functioning, the study of human relations *is* the curriculum.

THE WORLD OF WORK

Individual children can interview school employees—custodians, secretaries, aides, specialist teachers, classroom teachers, nurses, the principal—about their jobs. Children can plan their own questions for the interviews, or you can suggest some possibilities, for example: What do you like about your job? What do you dislike about it? How did you learn to do your job? If you were to change jobs, what else would you like to do? Why? Why do you think your job is important to the school? Similar interviews can be planned and conducted with various community residents, for example: firemen, policemen, gardeners, doctors, storekeepers, television repairmen, dressmakers, jewelers. Since such people are outside the school, these interviews involve more planning. Children can make their own arrangements with people who are friends or neighbors, and then bring the information to school for sharing. Children who conduct interviews can meet as a group to discuss and compare their findings. Some might even record the interview. Comparing and contrasting various jobs should create a respect for the importance of each.

This activity may also result in some expressed interest in exploring occupations that might appeal to individual children in the class. We are not suggesting the trite "What would you like to be?" approach, although even this has value, but interested children in a small group discussion can explore such questions as: Why do people work? What kind of work do you think you would like to do? Why? What jobs are there that you would like but think you could not do? Why? What jobs are you sure you would not like? Why? What are some things that you would consider before you chose your job? What kind of training will you need for the job you have selected?

Children might also want to discuss such things as the difference between a hobby and a job, and the values of each. Or they could talk about the kinds of jobs available today which were not available 100 years ago, and why. And, in reverse, they could discuss some jobs that were available 100 years ago that are no longer useful. (How about a blacksmith, a street-lamplighter, or a wagon driver?) Expanded discussions could include the question of which of today's jobs will still be necessary when the children become adults ready for the world of work. If you are studying a particular area of the world or a particular time in history, you could suggest an exploration and discussion of current jobs compared with jobs from another time or place. A good lead question might be, "Would the job you have selected for yourself be useful in _____[the area being studied] or would it have been useful when_____[another time in history]?"

Some children, in discussing their own job interests, might want to think and talk about the kinds of feelings they would have if they were especially successful at their particular job. Further discussions may develop about whether a feeling of having been a success can result from any job, for example:
When can a construction worker be satisfied and proud about his job? How about a garbage collector? a librarian? an astronaut? a salesman? a teacher? a plumber? a factory worker? a secretary?

Children could speculate about what might happen if the school custodian did not work for a week, or the garbagemen did not pick up the garbage, or the firemen decided not to work. Hopefully, they will develop a respect for all employment that makes some contribution to our society. Again, as in all open classroom activities, the uniqueness of each individual is emphasized.

SPECIAL TECHNIQUES FOR SPECIAL CHILDREN

For Slow Learners

Because teachers believe that all children can learn, materials and tasks must be provided for special children. "Special" can refer to the reluctant, disinterested, or shy child, as well as one with a low IQ and its attendant learning disabilities. Many of the ideas already presented can be used in teaching such children, but we would like to offer a few additional ideas to help meet the varied needs and abilities of this group. Whether the problem is physical or emotional, well-chosen activities, along with patience and encouragement, can help these children achieve some measure of success.

SUGGESTED TASKS

Use pictures, study prints, and all kinds of realia—samples of clothing, products, money, stamps, flags—for these children. Any objects that can be handled can supply a valuable kinesthetic learning experience. Art materials are also important, since through their use nonverbal children can express ideas about people and places being studied.

Peer teaching is an important aspect of all open classroom

activities; friends can help each other by sharing their talents and interests. Often a slower child has some special skill to share with a classmate who has greater academic skills. Many group projects need the artistic or manual talents that frequently belong to a child whose academic skills are limited. Make a point of using the known skills of these special children.

Audiovisual aids are a great help with slow learners. Filmstrips and records are good, and if your school has earphones, you can tape sections of books for children to use on cassettes. They can hear the tape several times, until they are satisfied with their understanding of it.

Simple dramatizations, including the use of puppets, can be worked out by groups of children that include slow learners. Often encouragement fosters greater efforts by these children to express themselves verbally.

Improvise simple learning games for these children. For example, you can make cards that indicate data to be matched (cities and countries, languages and countries, religions and countries, landmarks and cities), and invent rules similar to Old Maid or Rummy. You can also devise a Bingo game, using words from your social studies program.

For Gifted Children

Gifted children—those with high academic skills or special talents and interests—are a challenge to any classroom teacher, and the set-up of an open classroom certainly lends itself to meeting this challenge. Often, in a traditional classroom, these children's potential is limited by the structure of the program. Since they are often self-motivated, the enriched environment of your open classroom can be the means for fulfilling their needs. Peer teaching can provide many opportunities for gifted children to share their talents and skills with slower learners, and with children in lower grades.

SUGGESTED TASKS

Newspapers and newsmagazines present a challenge to children with high reading skills. They can meet in groups to discuss selected aspects of current problems presented in the news media, even analyzing some presentations critically.

Gifted children, individually or in groups, can assume responsibility for planning class or school bulletin board displays; they can collect, label, and arrange materials for exhibits related to a current social studies topic.

Gifted children who have a specific area of interest could be encouraged to do in-depth research, possibly extending over a long period of time, for example: biographies of interesting people and their influence upon other people's lives; a comparison of world religions, research into sports and games of different cultures; research into folk music and dancing; information about foreign currency and rates of exchange. Your library or media center specialist can help these children locate books and supplementary materials related to their specialized interests.

Emphasize the kinds of tasks suggested in the section on problem-solving. Gifted children respond readily to the challenge of situations involving relationships and requiring abstract thinking.

It is important to remember that gifted children and slow learners have many needs in common. Often their physical, social, and emotional growth are not at the same level as their mental development. Gifted children or slow learners should not be isolated with children of similar intellectual ability, since then the advantages of interaction and resulting understandings would be lost. One of the tasks of the teacher in an open classroom is to help children strike a balance in their activities, so that both individual activity and group involvements are meaningful learning procedures. In an open classroom, where we commit ourselves to serving the needs and desires of all children, certainly these "special" children deserve no less of our encouragement and support.

conclusion

To sum up, here are some keys to success in an open classroom: an enriched and constantly changing environment; freedom for each child to be a completely unique individual; acceptance by the child of responsibility for his own actions and accomplishments and those of the group. We believe that little or no learning takes place when the situations that children face in school have no meaning or interest for them. We also maintain that children have not only the right but the competence to make significant decisions about their own learning.

The three keys—enrichment, freedom, and responsibility—can help to open the doors to a happy and meaningful classroom experience for teachers and children. If educators are really searching for an educationally viable plan for teaching children, then they must commit themselves to procedures that encourage children to investigate the world around them in interesting and pleasurable ways. This is the essence of the open classroom.

We believe in the effectiveness of the open classroom. Though we can not advocate it as a panacea, we trust we have at least begun to convince you that it is relevant to many problems, as well as educationally sound. We also believe that a social studies program is exceptionally effective in an open classroom. We hope that you can use some of the ideas presented in this book to plan a productive open classroom that includes an exciting social studies program. Good luck!

ABOUT THE AUTHORS . . .

Evelyn Berger, a graduate of Montclair (N.J.) State College, has taught at the Lyncrest School in Fair Lawn, N.J., for more than a decade. Bonnie A. Winters, who is her daughter, was graduated from the University of Toledo in 1968 with a B.Ed., taught at the Maplewood School in Sylvania, Ohio, and received an M.Ed with a specialization in elementary social studies from Toledo in 1973.